HUMOR AND HEART

FROM THE HALLS OF ELEMENTARY SCHOOL

Sara Ajisafe

Principal Principles Publications

United States of America

Sara Ajisafe/Principal Principles Publications

HumorAndHeart@gmail.com

Ordering Information:

Quantity sales. Special discounts are available on quantity purchases by corporations, associations, and others. For details, contact the "Special Sales Department" at the address above.

Humor and Heart/ Sara Ajisafe. —1st ed.

ISBN 979-8-9987351-5-8 Paperback

ISBN 979-8-9987351-6-5 eBook

TABLE OF CONTENTS

DEDICATION

This book is dedicated first and foremost to God, to whom all things are possible. Every step of this journey exists because of His grace.

To my husband, **Toyin** — my constant, my steady beam of support. You have been on this education journey with me since the very beginning and are the one who inspired me to become a teacher in the first place. From late-night studying to helping me pick that quintessential first-day-of-school outfit, you have never wavered. Thank you for always believing in me, even when I questioned myself.

To my boys, **Azel and Zade** — you keep life fun, unpredictable, and full of purpose. You push me to chase my dreams and remind me daily that it is never too late to become who I'm meant to be.

To my siblings, **Mohamad, Hager, and Eman** — we share a bond that few could ever understand. At the end of the day, we love each other fiercely and are always cheering one another on.

To my dearest in-laws, **Femi and Modupe Ajisafe,** who have always loved me as a daughter. Your unconditional love, encouragement, and belief in me throughout all my endeavors have meant more than words can express.

To my sister-in-law, **Kahmahreeah,** my brother-in-law, **John,** and my cousin, **Heba** — thank you for your support on this creative journey in ways both big and small. Your behind-the-scenes love and effort did not go unnoticed. To my niece, **Riley**, thank you for helping edit videos and polish my social media posts; you keep me young and up to date.

To **Ron Clark**, who inspired me in February of 2020, just before the world changed. I was drawn to your charisma and your unwavering commitment to showing up for kids in unique and memorable ways. Visiting your academy remains one of the highlights of my career — a moment I often return to for inspiration.

To **Dr. B.**, my first principal as an assistant principal — thank you for pouring into me, believing in me, and being my biggest cheerleader. Your unwavering support shaped the leader I am today.

To **Mrs. Clark and Mr. Burns**, two principals who found me when my spirit was broken and, piece by piece, helped put me back together. Because of you, I rediscovered my joy, my confidence, and my peace.

To my **Mama and Baba** — none of this would be possible without you. Every idea, every dream, every leap of faith has been met with your encouragement and belief in me. I am forever grateful.

To my **#Sisterhood** — the first group of women I had the honor of serving as an assistant principal. Our first three years together were filled with laughter, growth, and countless lessons. No matter the distance or the state lines between us, you remain my people.

And finally, to **Stephanie**, my publisher — thank you for believing in this idea, trusting my voice, and being willing to try something new with me. Your support turned a collection of stories into a book, and for that, I am deeply grateful.

This book is because of all of you.

AUTHOR'S NOTE TO THE READER

After years in elementary schools, I've learned one undeniable truth: you truly can't make this stuff up.

Every day as an assistant principal, I've witnessed moments that made me laugh, cry, scratch my head, and occasionally question reality — often all before 10 a.m. The stories in this book are inspired by real events that unfolded within the colorful walls of elementary schools I've been lucky to serve.

Names, details, and identifying information have been changed (to protect the innocent... and the easily embarrassed), but the humor, heart, lessons learned, and honesty remain completely true.

This collection isn't just about the funny things kids say — though they are endless. It's also about well-meaning adults, creative problem-solving, the beautiful chaos, and the constant reminders that no two days in a school are ever the same.

Whether you're a teacher, parent, administrator, or anyone who's ever set foot in an elementary school, I hope these stories make you laugh, nod, and remember why schools are such magical, unpredictable places.

Because at the end of the day, education is part science, part art... and mostly comedy.

INTRODUCTION: FROM PUBLIC RELATIONS TO THE PRINCIPAL'S OFFICE

If you had told me years ago that I'd trade press releases for pencil sharpeners, or media pitches for morning announcements, I might have laughed. My career began in Public Relations — full of fast deadlines, glossy and non-glossy events, and carefully crafted messages. But somewhere along the way, life nudged me toward something far less predictable and infinitely more rewarding: elementary education.

Like any good story, my journey into schools started with curiosity and chaos. I went from managing client campaigns to managing classrooms, from writing speeches to writing lesson plans. And let me tell you — no PR crisis ever prepared me for a room full of third graders armed with glue sticks and opinions. I quickly learned that schools do not run on scripts. They run on unpredictability, honesty, and children who will say exactly what they're thinking — whether you're ready or not.

Over the years, I've had the privilege (and occasional shock) of working in elementary schools across three states and five school districts, serving as a classroom teacher, instructional coach, assistant principal, acting principal, and everything in between. No matter the zip code, the stories followed me. Different hallways. Same chaos. Same laughter. Same moments that made me pause and think, "did that really just happen?"

Along the way, I discovered that schools are places where joy and absurdity live side by side. Kids say things that could break the internet. Adults mean well, but sometimes miss the mark. And through it all, you either laugh or cry ... and I've done both, often in the same hour.

This book is a collection of those moments — the funny, awkward, honest, and deeply human stories that make working in schools unforgettable. Every story here is rooted in truth, told with affection, and shaped by the lessons that linger long after dismissal.

Because in the end, education isn't just about academics. It's about connection, resilience, and the laughter that keeps us going — one "you won't believe this" moment at a time.

You'll find stories about misunderstood emails, playground logic, bathroom investigations, first-grade philosophy, and lessons learned the hard way — like previewing every video, even when it's hosted by a child.

If you've ever worked in a school, sent your child to one, or simply wondered how educators keep it together when faced with tiny humans and very big emotions, this book is for you.

Welcome to the halls, the front office, the classrooms, and the moments in between.

The bell is about to ring...

— SARA AJISAFE

THE NURSE WHO ASKED

I was sitting in my principal's office when our school nurse stopped in, her expression serious. She leaned in and whispered, "Do you know what lice look like?"

For a second, we thought it was a trick question. The nurse was asking us — the principal and assistant principal — if we knew what lice looked like.

I blinked. "I was hoping you did," I said.

We all laughed, but at that moment, I realized: in schools, titles mean nothing when lice are involved. Suddenly, everyone's scratching their heads and Googling images like it's a medical emergency — because it usually is.

THE FINAL BELL

Sometimes, leadership isn't about having all the answers. It's about pretending you're not itching while you find them.

THE LADY IN THE BOOKSTORE

As acting principal one year, my attendance secretary came to me with an email that had just arrived from a parent, written entirely in Spanish. She ran it through a translator, looked at me wide-eyed, and read aloud:

"The lady in the bookstore spanked my daughter."

I froze. *The lady in the bookstore?* We didn't even have a bookstore.

Within minutes, we were piecing together clues like detectives — retracing schedules, checking coverage, and identifying every "lady" who had possibly interacted with this child. Eventually, we discovered that the "lady in the bookstore" was actually our media specialist — the sweetest human in the building — and that no one had been spanked.

At the time, students were engaged in independent stations throughout the media center. To keep traffic flowing smoothly, the Media Specialist had gently placed her arm around the student's shoulder to guide her back around the circulation desk. A small moment of redirection had turned into a full-scale mystery — all thanks to a translation app.

No crime. Just a bilingual misunderstanding with a touch of drama.

THE FINAL BELL:

Sometimes what gets lost in translation is our collective heartbeat returning to normal.

ONLY A BUSTED LIP

As an assistant principal in Texas, I once had a student involved in an altercation that left another child bleeding. When I sat down with the student to get their side of the story, they said confidently,

"She didn't say there was bleeding — only a busted lip."

I paused for a moment, torn between staying serious and wanting to burst out laughing. In this child's mind, a busted lip and bleeding were apparently two completely different medical conditions.

I tried to keep a straight face as I realized that, in the elementary world, technicalities are everything — especially when it comes to staying out of trouble.

THE FINAL BELL:

In the courtroom of elementary logic, "busted" and "bleeding" are not the same offense.

4

THE SCARY CLOWN

As an assistant principal, the principal and I received all kinds of parent requests — but one stands out above the rest.

One afternoon, a parent called and asked, in complete seriousness:

"Would it be okay if a scary clown came to school to surprise my child with flowers and cupcakes for their birthday?"

There was a long pause as we processed what we'd just heard... A scary clown... At school.

I pictured cupcakes flying, tears everywhere, and at least three kindergarteners needing counseling. Needless to say, we kindly suggested that perhaps the clown could make an appearance after dismissal.

THE FINAL BELL:

In elementary school, surprises are welcome — just maybe not the ones that come with face paint and a red balloon.

5

CHEW HER UP

As an assistant principal, I spent a lot of my days mediating playground dramas and friendship fallout. One afternoon, I was investigating a spat between two so-called friends — you know, the kind of argument that starts over a crayon and ends with life-long resentment.

I asked one student to explain what happened. She folded her arms, fixed me with a look usually reserved for serious villains in picture books, and said plainly:

"I can't even look at her. I just want to chew her up and spit her out."

For a beat, I was torn between being alarmed and being thoroughly impressed by the metaphor. Elementary school vocabulary: unexpectedly brutal, somehow poetic, and completely honest.

THE FINAL BELL:

Kids have a way of saying exactly what they mean — with metaphors that belong in a telenovela.

6

THE TACO INCIDENT

There once was a fight between two elementary boys — the classic tale of the boisterous kid who couldn't stop bothering the quiet, shy one. Day after day, the teasing continued until, finally, the quiet student had had enough and decided to fight back.

When the teacher called for assistance, I arrived to find the shy student uncharacteristically upset. After separating the two, I sat with him to talk. Through tears and frustration, he explained that the other student had been bothering him every day and that he simply couldn't take it anymore.

I felt his emotions so deeply in that moment — the quiet one who never caused trouble, finally breaking. Against all administrative logic, I found myself handing him my breakfast taco and telling him to take a breath before heading back to class.

Yes, I was that assistant principal — the one who technically rewarded bad behavior but also recognized a kid who just couldn't hold it in any longer.

THE FINAL BELL:

Sometimes justice looks less like a consequence... and sometimes more like a taco.

7

THE FAKE PIG

I've spent much of my time as an assistant principal talking with students about incidents that seem to happen most often during lunch or recess — the most unpredictable seventy minutes of any school day.

One afternoon, two students were sent to my office after an argument on the playground. Instead of having them talk it out, I decided to have each write down what happened. When they were done, I picked up the first student's paper and began to read.

It said:

"I had a pig — a fake one — and he said I got it from my ass."

I froze. My brain needed a full three seconds to process what I had just read. I wanted to laugh — truly, deeply laugh — but instead, I took a slow breath, nodded like this was a normal sentence, and began my calm talk about "appropriate language choices."

Inside, though, I was gone.

THE FINAL BELL:

Some days, professionalism is just keeping a straight face when the sentence makes absolutely no sense.

8

SOMETHING IS CONTROLLING ME

Often, students get sent to the office for disrupting the classroom — tapping pencils, making noises, or talking when they shouldn't. One day, a second grader walked in, clearly exasperated, and plopped down in the chair across from me.

I asked calmly, "Can you tell me why you were disrupting the class today?"

Without hesitation, and with complete sincerity, they said,

"Something is controlling me."

There was no smirk. No sarcasm. Just the honest belief that an external force — somewhere between science fiction and recess energy — had taken over their body.

I nodded slowly, fighting back a smile, and asked, "Do you think that something might give you back control so we can finish the day?" They agreed. Balance restored.

THE FINAL BELL:

In elementary school, accountability sometimes shares space with imagination.

9

THE NAP TIME INCIDENT

Ah, the joys of kindergarten — unpredictable, un-filtered, and 99.9% guaranteed to be the truth. You never know what you'll hear, but you can always count on it being said with full confidence.

One afternoon, I got the classic call: "There's been an incident during nap time." Those words alone can send shivers down any administrator's spine.

When I met with the alleged victim, I gently asked, "Can you tell me what happened?"

Without hesitation, the child replied,

"He was tickling my privates."

And there it was — five words that stopped time. No hesitation, no context, no filter. Just a statement of fact, delivered with kindergarten-level sincerity.

Inside, I was running through every possible next step while outwardly maintaining the calmest face of my career.

THE FINAL BELL:

Kindergarten truth-telling: pure, unedited, and always before you've had your second boost of caffeine.

WE'RE GOING TO SUE THAT SECOND-GRADER

Sometimes parents are more upset than the kids themselves, and in elementary school, that can make for some truly memorable conversations.

One afternoon, I had to call the family of a student who'd been hit by another child. The parent was understandably upset, and as I calmly explained the student code of conduct — without revealing any identifying details, of course — I heard a pause on the other end of the line.

Then the parent said, with complete seriousness, "We're going to sue that second grader."

I took a slow breath. I wanted to laugh, but instead, I thanked them for their time, reassured them we were addressing it, and hung up. Then I sat there picturing an 8-year-old in a tiny suit, standing before a judge, holding a juice box.

THE FINAL BELL:

Elementary school emotions are big — sometimes big enough to call a lawyer.

THE SUPER GLUE SALON

Two girls were sent to the office one afternoon for disrupting class. When they walked in, they looked nervous but oddly proud — the kind of look that says, "We might be in trouble, but we nailed it."

When I asked what had happened, their teacher explained they had been fidgeting with their nails instead of focusing on their work. I turned to the girls and asked, "What's going on with your nails?"

They looked at each other, then back at me, and confessed:

"We painted them with super glue."

I blinked. Super glue. Not polish. Not glitter. Super glue.

I wasn't sure whether to laugh or panic because I also had visions of the emergency room and permanent finger fusion. So instead, I calmly explained that while creativity is always encouraged, safety is the priority — and that super glue is not intended for use on the body.

THE FINAL BELL:

Elementary innovation knows no limits... or solvents.

1 2

THE TEACHER WITH THE CARTRIDGES

Many times, I receive parent concerns about something an adult allegedly said to a child. The tricky part? The child almost never knows the adult's name — only a vague description that turns the entire situation into a schoolwide guessing game.

One afternoon, I met with a student to gather more information. I asked calmly, "Can you tell me which teacher it was?"

The student thought for a moment and said with complete confidence,

"The teacher who has a hunchback and wears cartridges."

I blinked. Cartridges? It took me a solid minute — and a deep breath — before realizing they meant cardigans.

Mystery solved. Case closed. The teacher, thankfully, was just guilty of loving comfortable knitwear.

THE FINAL BELL:

In elementary school investigations, translation is everything — especially when "cartridges" are involved.

THE MONASTERY SCHOOL

During a meeting with a parent new to our school, my principal and I were learning more about their child's background. The parent began sharing, very matter-of-factly,

"He was at the monastery school."

My principal and I locked eyes — that silent educator telepathy that says, "Don't laugh, don't laugh, don't laugh."

After a long second of internal struggle, we realized the parent meant Montessori school. We nodded politely, still trying not to smile, and continued the conversation like nothing had happened.

THE FINAL BELL:

In education, pronunciation can make all the difference — monks and Montessori are two very different learning models.

A THOUSAND SPIDERS

One morning, the front office phone rang, and the secretary's eyes went wide. A kindergarten teacher was on the other end — frantic.

"There are precisely one thousand spiders in my classroom!" she exclaimed.

Without hesitation, the secretary called for backup. My principal and I dropped everything and sprinted down the hall, ready for battle — armed with nothing but bravery and a tissue box.

When we arrived, the teacher stood frozen by the door, pointing dramatically toward a corner of the room. We looked. We searched. We crouched.

Not a single spider in sight. Not one.

We reassured her the infestation had apparently relocated — and went back to our work, slightly out of breath and highly amused.

THE FINAL BELL:

In elementary school, emergencies range from paper cuts to plagues — and you never know which one you're running toward.

FIRST IMPRESSIONS

The beginning of the school year always brings exciting times — new faces, new routines, and a whole lot of introductions. When I started at a new elementary school, I made my way around to visit every classroom and introduced myself to the students.

Along the way, I received a series of unforgettable welcome messages from the most honest demographic on Earth: children.

A few highlights from the day:

- One student told me I smelled like sushi. (Still not sure if that was a compliment.)
- Another asked if I was married to Mr. Prin, the former Assistant Principal.
- One brave soul confidently announced, "I thought Mr. Prin got fired."
- And my personal favorite: "Can you stop asking me questions?"

Needless to say, first impressions were made — on both sides.

THE FINAL BELL:

Children are brutally honest, refreshingly curious, and occasionally ready to unionize against introductions.

THE BATHROOM INCIDENT

Ah, the occasional bathroom peeking incident — an inevitable part of elementary life that no administrator truly trains for.

One afternoon, a student reported that another classmate had been peeking through the bathroom stalls. With my best serious face on, I began the investigation. When I sat down with the alleged peeper to discuss what happened, he looked genuinely confused about why he was in trouble.

I asked, "Did you look under or through the stall?"

He replied earnestly,

"But I didn't see his wiener."

I had to take a deep breath — half to collect myself and half to stop the laughter threatening to escape. To him, that seemed like a perfectly reasonable defense.

THE FINAL BELL:

In elementary logic, intent matters... but apparently, so does visibility.

YOU HAVE POTENTIAL

On my journey toward the principalship, there have been plenty of bumps — lessons learned, goals reached, and moments that kept me grounded. I often like to ask kids big-picture questions, the kind that make them think beyond their world of recess and snack time.

One evening, I decided to ask my own elementary-aged child a reflective question:

"Do you think I'll ever become a principal?"

He paused thoughtfully, then replied,

"I don't know. Why are you asking me? Ask Dada — he knows about these things. But... you have potential."

And just like that, my pep talk came from the most honest coach I know.

THE FINAL BELL:

Sometimes the truest encouragement comes from little voices who don't even realize they're giving it.

HER NAME IS SPITFIRE

When little ones describe incidents or recall names, you quickly learn that accuracy takes a backseat to confidence. One afternoon, I was meeting with a student to follow up on a playground disagreement.

I asked gently, "Can you tell me who it was that said that to you?"

The student nodded seriously and replied,

"Her name is Spitfire."

I paused, mentally scrolling through every class list in the building — no Spitfire anywhere. After a few clarifying questions and one "aha" moment, I realized she meant Sapphire.

It was a completely innocent mix-up, delivered in the most serious tone imaginable, and I had to fight the urge to laugh.

THE FINAL BELL:

In elementary school storytelling, names may change — but the confidence in the delivery never does.

HALF GAY

One afternoon, a student came to me upset because another student had called them gay. As always, I wanted to get the full story, so I called the other student down to talk about what had happened.

When I asked them to explain, the student looked completely calm and said,

"But I only said they were half gay."

I blinked. Half. As if the fraction somehow softened the impact.

After taking a deep breath (and suppressing a laugh), we had a thoughtful conversation about respect, words, and how calling someone "half" of anything still means you're calling them that thing.

THE FINAL BELL:

Elementary math doesn't apply to kindness — fractions don't make name-calling any better.

THE CANDY INCIDENT

When I first started teaching at a charter school, I quickly became friends with the 4th- and 5th-grade teachers. One quiet afternoon, one of the 5th-grade teachers was sitting at her desk while her students worked silently. Suddenly, she heard a clatter — like the sound of beads scattering across the floor.

She stood up, walked to the back of the room, and saw candy everywhere. Or so she thought. When she bent down to pick it up, she froze.

They weren't candies. They were... tiny plastic penises. At least fifty of them.

Terrified, she scooped up as many as she could and ran straight down the hall to her colleague's classroom. Her friend opened the door, took one look, and burst into uncontrollable laughter.

Our principal, however, was not laughing. The teacher had to call every single parent whose child had come into contact with the "items." The parent of the student who had them was mortified. She explained that she had bought them for a bachelorette party and had no idea her child had taken them to school.

THE FINAL BELL:

Elementary surprises come in all shapes and sizes... some more educational than others.

THE BIKE PARK INCIDENT

In October of 2025, I had a very memorable weekend. My husband and I took our kids to the local bike park — and somewhere between cheering them on and wanting to prove I still had it; I decided to ride my nine-year-old's bike over the ramps.

I sailed over the first one like a pro. Then, as I stood to gain more speed for the second, I completely wiped out — full face plant. Blood was instantly running down my face. A trip to urgent care later confirmed it: broken nose, swollen lip, and one very bruised ego.

The next day, I showed up to work bandaged between my eyebrows, my upper lip twice its normal size. Naturally, the students were curious. A group of first graders gathered around and asked what happened. After I told them the story, one looked at me seriously and asked,

"Why would you do that? You're an adult — why would you ride a kid's bike?"

Another quickly chimed in,

"If I were an adult, I wouldn't do that."
And just like that, I was schooled — again.

THE FINAL BELL:

Leave it to first graders to remind you that wisdom doesn't always come with age... or training wheels.

THE GOVERNMENT SHUTDOWN VISIT

My husband works for the NIH, and on the first day of the 2025 government shutdown, I decided he needed a little pick-me-up. "Come have lunch with me," I told him. "You can see the new school I'm working at. Nothing cheers you up like smiling kids."

He agreed, so when he arrived, I gave him a tour of the building. As we walked down the hall, we passed a bubbly second-grade class. One very animated student noticed us and, with total amazement, exclaimed,

"That's your husband? He's Black, you're Black — I'm Black!"

There was a pause, and then she added proudly,

"My dad's Black."

I could barely hold it together. My husband smiled, the student beamed, and the moment was so wonderfully pure that it instantly turned his gloomy day around.

THE FINAL BELL:

Children remind us that sometimes joy lives in the simplest observations — and the most unexpected hallways.

YOU DON'T HAVE TO GO

One afternoon, our special education teacher walked into a first-grade classroom to work with a small group of students. As she entered, the class got quiet — all eyes watching.

When the special educator called the name of the student she was there to support, another classmate turned, looked them straight in the eye, and said confidently,

"You know you don't have to go with her if you don't want to."

Completely serious. Completely sincere.

The special educator and the classroom teacher locked eyes, both doing their best not to laugh. It was a simple statement — part empathy, part rebellion — and entirely first grade.

THE FINAL BELL:

Elementary friendships run deep... especially when it comes to rescuing each other from small-group instruction.

PREVIEW EVERYTHING

In my first year of teaching, I was a career switcher coming from the world of Public Relations — and let's just say the learning curve was steep. I was teaching third grade, determined to make every lesson engaging and meaningful.

During a unit on slavery, I found what seemed like the perfect video: it was hosted by a child, so naturally I thought, "It's kid-friendly — no need to preview."

Halfway through, during a scene between a slave and a slave owner, the owner suddenly shouted,

"You damned bitch!"

The class gasped. I froze for a millisecond, then launched myself toward the computer like an Olympic sprinter to hit "stop." The damage was done — thirty shocked faces staring back at me.

Lesson learned: preview everything. Even if it's hosted by a kid. Especially if it's hosted by a kid.

THE FINAL BELL:

Teaching will humble you — sometimes in three seconds flat and in front of an entire class of third graders.

IT'S GIVING YOGURT

It was early spring, and I had gathered our fifth-grade safety patrols for a meeting. The air was full of sunshine, optimism, and pollen — which may explain why I had started leaning into brighter, bolder colors. That day, I wore a long-sleeve top with purple and yellow stripes — both horizontal and vertical — feeling very fresh season, fresh energy.

After the meeting, one student looked me up and down with the kind of thoughtful expression usually reserved for art critiques. Then, with complete seriousness, he said,

"It's giving yogurt."

I blinked. Yogurt.

"Like a Go-Gurt?" I asked.

He nodded, and we both burst out laughing.

I smiled and thanked him for the... feedback.

THE FINAL BELL:

In elementary fashion, if you're lucky, you'll serve looks — but some days, you just serve snacks.

FRIENDS ON OCTOBER 21

I love spending time down in the kindergarten hall — it's unpredictable, full of energy, and always guaranteed to make you laugh. One morning, I was making my rounds, greeting students as they arrived.

A little one stopped me and announced, "They won't be my friend."

I knelt down to listen and gently reminded her, "We're friends with everyone here."

She shook her head and said firmly, "But she's not my friend."

I turned to the other student and asked, "Aren't you friends with her?"

With total seriousness, she replied,

"On October 21."

I chuckled softly, careful not to encourage the drama, and said, "We're friends on all days." Later, I shared the story with the kindergarten teachers, and we laughed until we cried. Apparently, friendship in kindergarten runs on an appointment basis.

THE FINAL BELL:

In kindergarten, friendships are precious, dramatic, and — occasionally — scheduled.

BUT WAIT, WHO ARE YOU?

For Halloween, my principal and I decided to go all in and dress as Taylor Swift and Travis Kelce. I had the sparkles, the confidence, and the playlist — ready to make the rounds and spread some pop-star energy through the hallways.

As I made my way around the school, one very excited second grader saw me coming and began jumping up and down, squealing,

"OMG! I love Taylor Swift!"

I matched her energy, jumping up and down too, and said, "Me too!"

Then she suddenly stopped, got very serious, tilted her head, and said,

"But wait... who are you?"

In that instant, I realized she didn't recognize me at all.

"Baby," I laughed, "it's me — Mrs. Ajisafe!"

She blinked and replied simply,

"Oh."

And just like that, my pop-star moment was over.

THE FINAL BELL:

Kids will keep you humble — no matter how good your costume (or your era).

WHY DIDN'T YOU CLEAN MY CUT?

One day during kindergarten recess, a student scraped her knee and came running to me with big tears in her eyes. I gently brought her over to the recess cart, made sure it was clean, and put a bandage on it.

I didn't send her to the nurse — because in elementary school, the nurse's cleaning toolkit consists of exactly one approved item: water. No peroxide, no alcohol, no Neosporin... nothing. Just water and a silent prayer.

The next morning at the bus loop, she hopped off the bus, marched right up to me, and announced,

"Why didn't you clean my cut?"

I explained, "Baby, we can't clean it with anything at school, only water."

She stared at me like I had broken every medical law known to man.

THE FINAL BELL:

In kindergarten healthcare, expectations are high — and the approved supply list is not.

HE TRIES TO TWERK ON US

Two younger-grade students were sent to my office to report an issue with a boy in their class. They walked in with the seriousness of detectives ready to present a case. I sat down across from them and gently asked, "What's going on?"

Both girls looked at each other, then at me, and with complete sincerity said,

"When we're trying to do our work... he tries to twerk on us."

I blinked. Of all the sentences I expected to hear that day, that was not even in the top one hundred.

After collecting myself, I thanked them for telling me, assured them we would address it, and began preparing for one of the more unique behavioral conversations of my career.

THE FINAL BELL:

In elementary school, even dance moves can become office referrals.

THE LONGEST SILENCE

I once had a student sent to my office for using inappropriate language. When I asked what they said, the student went completely silent. Not a word.

I reassured them, "That's fine — I can wait until you're ready."

So, we sat. And sat. And sat.

Eventually, boredom won over stubbornness, and the student finally blurted out a rhyme — an extremely creative, extremely inappropriate rhyme — involving various body parts being compared to food and noodles.

I had to hold my breath to keep from reacting. I thanked them for finally telling me, talked about appropriate language and choices... and then immediately walked into my office and closed the door so I could collect myself.

THE FINAL BELL:

Silence may be golden, but sometimes what breaks it is unforgettable.

PLEASE WRITE IT DOWN

A student was once sent to my office for calling another student a "T.H.O.T." At the time, I had absolutely no idea what that meant — zero. But of course, as the adult in charge, I couldn't say that.

So, I nodded thoughtfully, leaned forward, and began gently pressing the student with questions, hoping context clues would save me. No luck.

I finally said, "Why don't you write down what that means for me?" handing over a sticky note like it was part of the official investigation process.

The student wrote carefully, then handed it back. The note said:

"A person who meets a lot of people, such as males or females."

I stared at the definition — equal parts relieved, amused, and still slightly confused — and launched into a conversation about respectful language and choosing words that lift people up instead of putting them down.

THE FINAL BELL:

In elementary school discipline, sometimes the sticky note teaches the adult just as much as the child.

WE'RE HELPING HIM

At the end of lunch duty one afternoon, I noticed two very cute first graders, each holding the hand of another classmate. As someone who has learned to anticipate unusual situations, I walked over to see what was going on and why they felt the need to escort him.

I smiled and asked, "Hey guys, what's going on here?"

Without hesitation, and with the purest sincerity imaginable, they said,

"He's special needs. We're helping him get outside for recess."

I paused — not because the moment wasn't kind, but because it was clear their hearts were in exactly the right place, even if their words weren't quite there yet. What they meant was that their classmate needed a little extra support, and they wanted to help — which, in first-grade terms, is about as compassionate as it gets.

We talked briefly about how everyone needs help sometimes and how we can be kind without labeling people. Then I thanked them for being such good friends and sent them off to recess, still holding hands.

THE FINAL BELL:

Kids may not always have the language — but their kindness usually speaks first.

WHAT KIND OF PAJAMAS ARE THOSE?

Ahhh, the infamous Spirit Week — a beloved tradition for students and a strategic wardrobe challenge for administrators. Without fail, it always includes Pajama Day... my least favorite. In case of an emergency, I prefer to look at least somewhat put together, so instead of true pajamas, I opt for a matching sweatsuit. Cozy, comfortable—but still: "I can lead an evacuation if necessary."

One morning, I was visiting a kindergarten classroom in my coordinated, non-pajama pajama alternative. A little fellow looked me dead in the eyes and said, with total seriousness,

"What kind of pajamas are those?"

And just like that, I was exposed.

THE FINAL BELL:

Kindergarteners don't care about safety plans or dress codes — if it's Pajama Day, you'd better commit.

THE DEAD RAT EMAIL

Nothing evokes more panic in an administrator than opening an email from a parent that starts with:

"My child said the recess monitor told them to pick up a dead rat."

My heart dropped. Cue the investigation. Cue the camera footage. Cue me mentally drafting apologies while also trying to figure out who on staff would EVER give such a directive.

After reviewing the footage, here's what actually happened:

The student picked up the dead rat.

With his water bottle.

Held it up proudly and brought it to the recess monitor.

The recess monitor — horrified — told him to throw it away immediately and go wash his hands.

Case solved.

No staff misconduct.

Just an adventurous child, a deceased rodent, and a very misleading retelling.

THE FINAL BELL:

In elementary school, the truth is usually stranger — and significantly more unsanitary — than the original complaint.

I DIDN'T TOUCH FOR REAL

I was called to investigate the classic elementary complaint:

"They touched my private parts."

Never a fun sentence to hear, but always one that requires immediate attention. I brought the two students to my office to talk through what happened.

One student explained, "I just poked him on the butt."

The other student confirmed this version — which was not the alarming story originally shared with the Paraeducator on lunch duty.

After lots of clarifying questions and careful listening, I finally turned to the student accused of poking and asked, "Can you tell me exactly what you did?"

He looked at me very seriously and said,

"I didn't touch for real."

That launched us into a conversation about how any touching — even a "not for real" touch — is still touching, and that our classroom and playground rules apply whether they consider it "for real" or not.

THE FINAL BELL:

In elementary school, logic comes in many forms — but "not for real" still counts.

I WAS GOING TO TREAT THEM

I was called to handle a situation involving four first graders — one of whom was said to have threatened three classmates. It all began in the cafeteria when a student threw his lunchbox into the air. The paraeducator caught him and reminded him not to do it again.

Naturally, in perfect first-grade fashion, he did it again.

Caught again.

This time, the paraeducator told him he would lose five minutes of recess.

Apparently, this consequence ignited something within him, because while the class lined up, he went up to three peers and announced that after his five penalty minutes:

"I'm going to fight you."

I went to visit him in class to talk through what happened. He looked at me and said very seriously,

"I was going to threat them."

I blinked.

"You were going to... What does 'threat them' mean?"

He explained matter-of-factly:

"I was making a list of students to chase and fight after the five minutes."

That was enough of that conversation — so I went to get the three "threatened" students. I brought them to an empty room to hear their side. They confirmed the entire saga: the lunchbox toss, the consequence, the declaration of future battle.

Great — story confirmed, consequences assigned.

When we finished, I said, "Okay, thanks for sharing. Let's head back to class."

One of the students looked around the quiet, empty room, sighed dramatically, and said:

"I feel like I wanna stay here."

We all burst out laughing.

THE FINAL BELL:

Some days, solving the conflict is easy — it's convincing them to go back to class that's the real challenge.

NOT THAT COOKIE

My current school was awarded a Blue Ribbon, and with that came a wave of celebrations. One of the treats included embroidered quarter-zip sweaters for every staff member and a custom cookie designed to match the Blue Ribbon logo.

The PTA sponsored the cookies and asked me to take photos of staff holding them. After making my rounds, I returned to the front office and told the secretaries, "Okay, your turn! I need to take your picture with your cookies."

One of the secretaries looked down into her lap, confused, and said:

"My cookie?"

I burst out laughing.

"No — not that cookie! The one the PTA gave us!"

We all cracked up for a solid minute.

THE FINAL BELL:

In schools, communication is key — especially when cookies are involved.

HE CIRCLED GLAD

A first grader had called another student "gay," so I brought the student in to complete a reflection sheet — our age-appropriate way of helping kids think through their actions.

One of the questions on the sheet listed a range of feelings:

Glad, sad, worried, confused, mad, tired, frustrated, or afraid.

The student circled "glad."

I paused.

"You were glad about what happened?" I asked.

He nodded confidently.

"...You're happy that you called someone that?" I clarified gently.

Again, total certainty: "Yes."

"Why?" I asked, bracing myself.

He shrugged and said,

"Because they were laughing."

And just like that, it became clear — the entire meaning of the word had gone straight over his first-grade head.

THE FINAL BELL:

In elementary school, intent and understanding are rarely on the same page — especially when everyone is laughing.

THE CANDLE ON THE CHROMEBOOK CART

Most mornings, I make my rounds through each classroom — saying hello to students, checking in with teachers, and getting a feel for the school's vibe. It's one of the best parts of my day.

On this particular morning, I walked into a first-grade classroom and immediately noticed something... concerning. The teacher — who was definitely not new to the profession — had a real candle burning.

On top of a Chromebook cart.

A cart filled with cords, devices, batteries, and everything else on the "please don't set this near open flames" list.

I stood there, shocked.

She cheerfully carried on.

The candle kept burning until she was told to blow it out.

You truly cannot make this stuff up.

THE FINAL BELL:

Experience doesn't always equal judgment — especially when décor meets technology.

THE LEGGINGS INCIDENT

At a staff meeting one afternoon, I sat quietly observing everyone as they came in — taking attendance in my head, reading the room, doing what administrators do.

Then my eyes landed on one teacher.

She was wearing extremely tight leggings, the kind that leave very little to the imagination. And let's just say... her undergarments were not cooperating. There was bunching, twisting, and a very visible outline that I could not unsee once I had seen it.

I found myself wondering — did her students notice this?

If I can see it from across the room, surely a class of curious, unfiltered children has commented at least once.

I spent the next few minutes trying (and failing) not to laugh to myself.

THE FINAL BELL:

In education, some things you can address and some things... you just pray the kids don't point out.

A TINY ACCIDENT

A first grader was sent to the office for hitting another student, but I happened to be in a meeting with my principal. So, he waited... and waited... and waited.

At one point, he told one of the secretaries,

"It's taking too long, and I'm getting mad."

Eventually, the admin secretary returned to the office and said, "There's a first grader waiting for you."

"Send him back," I said.

He walked in, sat down, and I asked gently, "Can you tell me what happened?"

With total sincerity, he replied:

"I did a tiny accident. It was on a total accident."

After a little more talking, he finally admitted that he had hit another student — but assured me confidently that he had

"Learned his lesson."

THE FINAL BELL:

In first grade, accountability is a journey — and every mistake starts as "a tiny accident."

CVS OR CPS?

Having many educator friends means we often exchange the funniest — and sometimes most eyebrow-raising — stories. One colleague shared a moment that perfectly captures the innocence of children mixed with the very real responsibilities of school life.

During class, a student casually told their teacher:

"My mom said I can't tell you anything because you'll call CVS on her."

The teacher froze.

CVS?

It took a moment to realize the child meant CPS — a very serious agency with very serious implications.

The innocence in the mispronunciation was hilarious...

The root of the statement?

Not funny at all.

But that's the reality of working in schools — moments that swing from adorable to heavy in the blink of an eye.

THE FINAL BELL:

Kids confuse the acronyms — adults never confuse the responsibility.

DO YOU THINK MY DAD IS HANDSOME?

During dismissal one afternoon, a former colleague was helping students get to their cars when a child walked up proudly and asked:

"Do you like my dad's shirt?"

The teacher smiled and said, "Yes, it's very nice."

Then came the follow-up question — the kind that only kids ask without warning:

"Do you think my dad is handsome?"

There was a long pause, a careful glance, and finally, an "Uhhhhh... sure."

The student nodded thoughtfully and delivered the twist of the century:

"Well, he likes someone else."

And with that, dismissal turned into a small soap opera.

THE FINAL BELL:

Elementary conversations can go from fashion review to family drama in under ten seconds.

44

TELL HER TO LEAVE ME ALONE

Sometimes students need extra one-on-one support during the school day — for focus, emotional regulation, or just a little extra guidance. In this case, a first grader had their paraeducator working closely with them when the classroom teacher came over to check in.

Before the teacher could even speak, the student turned to their paraeducator and said, with full first-grade attitude:

"Can you tell that... stupid ass bitch to leave me alone?"

The delivery was so unexpectedly bold that every adult in the room had to summon every ounce of professionalism not to react. We were all silently dying on the inside.

After a moment, we regrouped, redirected, and moved on — but the moment definitely lived on in our collective memory.

THE FINAL BELL:

In elementary school, tiny voices can deliver very big statements — often when you least expect them.

RUNWAY READY

One morning, a kindergartener arrived at school looking like she had stepped straight off a very creative runway. She had self-painted eyebrows — bold, dark, and dramatically uneven — and lipstick that was not so much on her lips as it was around her entire mouth like a bright, confident halo.

She strutted in with complete pride, backpack bouncing, absolutely unbothered by the fact that she looked like she had gotten ready in a moving vehicle during an earthquake.

And honestly? She was adorable.

THE FINAL BELL:

In kindergarten, confidence beats technique every time.

THE BALD-HEADED REPUBLICAN

Students will often come to the office to report something an adult said or did that they feel was unfair. One afternoon, a student arrived with great urgency to tell me about an interaction they felt had been very unjust.

I started with the usual questions:

"What did they say?"

"Who was it?"

The student paused, thinking hard. They couldn't remember the adult's name — just that the person was a visitor in the building that day.

Finally, with complete seriousness and total confidence, they said:

"It was the bald-headed Republican."

I blinked.

"How do you know they were a Republican?" I asked gently.

They were adamant.

No doubt in their mind.

That was the best descriptor they had.

And truly? It was one of the most specific, unhelpful, and hilarious identifiers I've ever received.

THE FINAL BELL:

Elementary reporting relies less on facts and more on whatever detail sticks — even political party guesses.

LITTLE BLACK THINGS

No one ever likes being sent to the Principal's or Assistant Principal's office — especially when they're there for causing a problem. On this particular day, I was doing my usual routine, asking all the standard questions to piece together what had happened.

But I wasn't getting much.

Lots of shrugs.

Lots of silence.

Lots of looking everywhere except at me.

After what felt like an eternity of gentle prompting, the student finally looked up, wide-eyed, and said—

"Little black things are flying around."

I blinked.

Was this... a horror film gone wrong?

Were we entering a new dimension of distraction techniques?

I had no idea what "little black things" were, but I knew one thing for sure — we had officially left the realm of logical explanations.

THE FINAL BELL:

In elementary discipline, you expect excuses — but some days, you get special effects.

THE LITTLE CLIMBER

A former colleague of mine taught kindergarten and had a particularly rambunctious little girl who loved climbing anything she could get her hands on. One afternoon at dismissal, the teacher saw her trying to scale the wall and called out:

"Hey, little climber, come down from there!"

The student hopped down, turned around, and said proudly,

"My dad calls me a monkey when I climb the stripper pole at home."

The teacher froze.

The child continued cheerfully, explaining that her parents had a pole in their bedroom.

It took every ounce of professionalism not to react.

Just another day in kindergarten.

THE FINAL BELL:

Kids will tell you everything — especially the things you never, ever expected or wanted to hear.

49

THE SHINY BALD HEAD

It was our annual Open House Day — the one where families flood the building, eager to peek into classrooms and catch a glimpse of their child's school world. In one first-grade class, we'd been having on-going challenges with a particularly grumpy parent. Naturally, as an administrator, that made me a little anxious. The last thing any of us needed was to give him new material to be upset about.

When the class transitioned to Art, their special education teacher went with them — and so did the dad. I watched from a distance as they walked by, just keeping an eye on things.

As soon as they entered the Art room, one very spirited student took one look at the dad and shouted for the entire class (and teacher... and parent) to hear:

"Look at that man with the shiny bald head!"

There was a beat of silence — and then the entire class burst into laughter.

Everyone... except the dad.

He remained stone-faced, arms crossed, not even the tiniest smile.

Meanwhile, the rest of us were doing our best to look not amused while absolutely dying on the inside.

THE FINAL BELL:

Kids don't mean to roast people — but when they do, they do it with honesty, volume, and impeccable timing.

THAT'S A STUPID NAME

On the first day of the government shutdown — the same day my husband came to visit my school for a little pick-me-up — our school director happened to walk by my office. As they passed, I quietly leaned over to my husband and said:

"That's" a name that rhymes with "jerk."

What I didn't take into account was my first-grade visitor, who was sitting in my office with us.

Without missing a beat, the student confidently chimed in—

"Jerk? That's a stupid name."

My husband and I froze... then immediately burst out laughing.

I quickly corrected him, of course — but we absolutely enjoyed the moment of unexpected comedy.

THE FINAL BELL:

Little ears hear everything... and little mouths repeat it with boldness you never see coming.

AT HOME BAKING

During COVID, while students learned from home, administrators were still expected to report to the building. The hallways were silent, classrooms empty, but the work kept going. I used the quiet to catch up on tasks and make a few parent phone calls.

One afternoon, I called a dad to check in about his child. He answered, clearly surprised to hear from anyone at the school. After a brief pause, he said:

"Oh! I thought you'd be at home... baking."

I blinked.

Baking?

Was that what he imagined educators did during a pandemic?

I laughed and explained that administrators were still reporting to the building. Although I suspected he was being serious!

But the image stuck with me — me in an apron, whisking batter, instead of handling attendance data and Zoom troubleshooting.

THE FINAL BELL:

In a crisis, everyone imagined educators doing something different — but baking was definitely not in the job description.

SOMETIMES, I BLACK OUT

It's the same old story — a student gets sent to the office for causing trouble. I bring them in, offer a patient ear, and begin the familiar dance of gentle questioning.

At first, I get vague answers.

Then partial answers.

Then entirely new versions of the truth I've never heard before.

We work our way through multiple retellings — each one slightly different — until we finally begin to land on what actually happened.

And just when I think we're getting somewhere, the student looks at me with complete sincerity and says—

"Sometimes... I black out."

I paused, trying not to laugh.

"Black out?" I asked gently.

They nodded solemnly, as though delivering a medical diagnosis.

And that was the moment I knew: we had officially entered the realm of elementary-level dramatic flair.

THE FINAL BELL:

In student interviews, the truth comes eventually — but the plot twists come first.

I NEED TO CHANGE MY PAD

You know that feeling when your walkie crackles and you hear, "We need an administrator to room 120"?

Every administrator's heart skips a beat.

Is it a medical emergency?

A behavior crisis?

A parent situation?

You hustle down the hallway, preparing for anything.

Well... almost anything.

I arrived at the classroom ready for a full-scale crisis. The teacher met me at the door, completely calm, and said:

"Can you watch my class? I need to go change my pad."

I froze.

That was... not on my list of anticipated emergencies.

But there I was — stepping in, greeting the students, and trying not to laugh at the absolute honesty of it all.

Just another day in the life.

THE FINAL BELL:

In elementary schools, emergencies come in all forms — and sometimes, they're refreshingly straightforward.

OH, I AM?

I once met with a student about an inappropriate word she had used during recess. As we talked, I explained why the word was hurtful and how language can have a real impact. I tried to give an example that would resonate with her personally, so I said gently, "You're Asian, so imagine if someone said—"

Before I could finish, she stopped me mid-sentence, eyes wide, and said:

"Oh, I am?"

I smiled.

"Yes, honey. India is part of Asia."

She nodded slowly, processing this brand-new piece of identity-defining information.

We paused the behavior conversation for a quick geography lesson — and then continued.

THE FINAL BELL:

Sometimes the teachable moment isn't the one you planned — but the one they didn't know they needed.

TOO MUCH COFFEE

Another classroom emergency came over the walkie — the kind that required an administrator to report immediately. I hustled down the hallway, always prepared for anything from a behavior crisis to a medical situation.

When I arrived, the teacher met me at the door and said, completely straight-faced:

"I drank too much coffee, and now my heart is racing. I need to go lie down."

She casually added that she had medication for this condition — in her car — but it wasn't urgent enough to go get it.

So, I stepped in to watch her class while she went to lie down in the nurse's office. Meanwhile, my mind was spinning.

1. She knew this happened when she drank too much coffee... and drank all that coffee anyway.

2.   She had medication... and didn't think retrieving it was worth the walk to the parking lot.

I stayed with her very calm group of students and tried to process the situation without letting my face show what I was thinking.

THE FINAL BELL:

Sometimes the adults need supervising just as much as the kids — and coffee is a powerful villain.

THEY TASTE THE SAME

Our PE coach was reviewing the day's lesson with his first graders — talking about exercise, our bodies, and why we sweat. Simple, harmless science.

Then one very serious student raised their hand and asked:

"Are sweat and pee the same thing?"

The coach blinked and said, "No... why?"

Without hesitation, the student replied:

"Because they taste the same."

There was a moment — a brief, stunned silence — as the coach's entire life flashed before his eyes.

And then, the class carried on as if nothing had happened.

Meanwhile, every adult who heard the story later needed a full minute to recover.

THE FINAL BELL:

In first grade, questions are innocent... answers are not always comforting.

I LIKE TO DRINK MY BLOOD

During one of my morning visits to a first-grade classroom, a bright-eyed, very energetic student stopped me with the kind of urgency that usually means someone lost a tooth or brought in a dead bug.

Instead, she looked up at me and announced proudly—

"I like to drink my blood."

I blinked.

"...What?"

She held up her finger and explained that she'd had a small cut. As it was bleeding, she'd been sucking on it. And then — with complete confidence — she added:

"I like the taste."

I stood there, trying to keep my face neutral while internally processing far too much information for 9:15 a.m.

She, meanwhile, went right back to her morning work like she had simply shared her favorite ice cream flavor.

THE FINAL BELL:

Kids tell you the truth — even when you're not remotely prepared for the truth they choose.

INSIDE-OUT

In my first year as an assistant principal, I was also working with a first-year fifth-grade teacher. It was both of our first years in new roles — so, naturally, there were plenty of bumps along the way. To make matters more interesting, my office happened to be directly across from the staff bathroom.

You would not believe how many times someone forgot to lock that door... and how many accidental walk-ins occurred. It became an unfortunate rite of passage.

One afternoon, I was working at my desk when this sweet first-year teacher came flying out of the bathroom and announced, loud and proud:

"I'm wearing my underwear inside out!"

I looked up, shocked, and asked, "Everything okay?"

We locked eyes — and immediately burst into uncontrollable laughter.

And this, believe it or not, was only the first of three times this exact situation happened to her.

First years in any school position are not for the faint of heart.

THE FINAL BELL:

In your first year, you're just trying to survive — sometimes even your laundry is confused.

YOUR PANTS ARE LOSING THE FIGHT

In my first year as an assistant principal, I was still learning how to balance being direct with being compassionate. It's a skill you refine over time — sometimes through very memorable moments.

One afternoon, I spotted one of our younger teachers walking down the hallway. Her pants were clearly doing her no favors and had completely lost the battle with gravity. Without thinking — truly without one ounce of professional filtering — I blurted out:

"Your butt is eating your pants."

She froze.

Looked at me.

Then burst out laughing.

Thank goodness she was not offended. We both laughed so hard that I'm sure anyone watching thought we were losing our minds in the hallway.

It was one of those moments I replayed in my head later, thinking—

Wow. First-year admin-me really had no internal editor.

THE FINAL BELL:

Growth sometimes begins the moment after you say the thing you absolutely should have kept in your head.

THE WRONG HAPPY MEAL

It was a super busy day, and when I stepped out of my office, I noticed a Happy Meal sitting on the counter waiting to be delivered. I asked the secretary who it belonged to, but she couldn't quite remember the name — she offered a few guesses, none of which felt right.

So, the search began.

I went down to the cafeteria to see if any kindergartners were missing a lunch.

Nope — every child had food.

I asked the paraeducators if anyone was expecting a special birthday lunch.

Nope — no clues there either.

I went back to the office and reported that everyone seemed accounted for.

The secretary thought for a second, then suddenly lit up and confidently announced the student's name:

"It belongs to him— [student's name]; it's his birthday!"

Perfect. Mystery solved.

I rushed back to the cafeteria, found the student, delivered the Happy Meal, and cheerfully wished him Happy Birthday! He smiled politely, and I went on with my day.

A few minutes later, the lunch monitor came into the office looking puzzled.

She said:

"He says he doesn't eat this."

And then it hit me — the student was Indian and a practicing Hindu.

I gasped, "Oh my gosh — did he eat it?"

She replied, "He took one tiny bite and said he didn't like it."

I said, "Go tell the secretary! She told me to give it to him!"

Later, when the secretary shared the story with the principal, he asked:

"Well... who gave him the burger?"

We were all laughing when the answer — of course — was:

"Sara did."

Don't worry — I immediately called the family to explain the mix-up, and they were gracious and understanding.

And the Happy Meal?

It belonged to a second grader the entire time.

THE FINAL BELL:

Sometimes the busiest days lead to the biggest mix-ups — and even the best intentions can take you on an unexpected Happy Meal adventure.

THE WRONG SECRET PAL

Ah, the good ol' Secret Pal tradition — the anonymous gift exchange that brings joy, suspense, and the occasional identity crisis. At my current school, we start in September and run it straight through Winter Break.

In the first week of December, I was delivering items to teacher mailboxes. A teacher happened to be in the mailroom, so I casually asked:

"What's so-and-so's last name again?"

She told me.

I froze.

"Wait... what?"

Because suddenly, it all clicked.

I had been putting my Secret Pal's gifts in the wrong mailbox since September.

SAME last name.

One with an S, one without.

We both burst out laughing — because of course something like this would happen in December, the Super Bowl of school chaos.

I ended up confessing to my real Secret Pal and explaining why she hadn't received anything all fall. Needless to say, her winter gift included a very generous gift card to make up for the accidental three-month drought.

THE FINAL BELL:

In a school full of identical last names, even Secret Santa needs a seating chart.

THE AFTER-SCHOOL WAXING SALON

Desperate times call for desperate measures — and as a first-year teacher living on a first-year teacher salary, I became resourceful very quickly. One of my proudest (and now slightly alarming) DIY talents was learning how to wax my own legs and armpits.

Word travels fast in a school, and once my colleagues found out I could wax, suddenly I had a line of teachers after school asking for help.

Before I knew it, my classroom — the same room where students learned reading and math — had transformed into an informal, after-hours waxing salon. I had teachers coming in with rolled-up sleeves, pant legs pulled halfway up, and lots of "Okay, just count to three..."

Looking back, I cannot believe I was doing beauty treatments in the middle of my classroom, like it was completely normal. But honestly? We had so much fun, and everyone left a little smoother and a lot more entertained.

P.S. No private parts were EVER waxed — that would've required hazard pay!

THE FINAL BELL:

In education, creativity isn't just for lesson plans — sometimes it's for survival (and smoother arm-pits).

THE SILLY STRING REVENGE

It's the classic story: girl chases boy on the playground, boy wants absolutely nothing to do with being chased. Instead of ignoring her or running faster, this boy chose a far more... creative approach.

He grabbed a can of silly string from home and brought it to school the next day. After recess, he marched straight to her locker.

Then, with the confidence of a cartoon villain, he sprayed the entire thing out — top to bottom, corner to corner, not a surface left untouched.

Locker.

Coat.

Backpack.

Lunchbox.

You name it — it had silly string on it.

By the time we discovered the scene, it looked like a party store had exploded inside her cubby.

Of course, consequences followed. With parent permission, he spent part of his recess the next day helping to clean several lockers — a hands-on lesson in respecting other people's things.

THE FINAL BELL:

In elementary school, romance is complicated — and revenge comes in neon foam.

THE 100ᵀᴴ DAY ASSAULT RIFLES

The 100th day of school is a major celebration in kindergarten. Teachers get creative, kids bring in collections of 100 items, and many proudly wear shirts decorated with 100 objects — buttons, stickers, googly eyes... You name it.

On this particular 100th day, I spotted a kindergartner walking proudly in a black shirt covered in 100 white drawings. From across the room, I couldn't quite tell what they were, so I made my way closer to admire his design.

And then I froze.

They were 100 tiny assault rifles hand-drawn across the entire shirt.

I blinked.

 Once.

 Twice.

At dismissal, I stopped by his classroom to speak with his parent, gently explaining that the shirt was inappropriate for school.

The parent smiled and said:

"Oh, he made it with his dad."

As if that explained everything.

I thanked them for listening and encouraged a more school-friendly approach next year.

THE FINAL BELL:

In kindergarten, creativity is endless — and sometimes the grown-ups need more precise directions.

GRANNY AND THE NYQUIL

At one of my former schools, we had a wonderful program where elderly community members came in to volunteer in classrooms. They were affectionately known as our grannies and grandpas, and the kids adored them. They brought warmth, patience, and a little bit of old-school charm to our hallways.

One morning, a second-grade teacher called the office asking for an administrator. I headed down, expecting a behavior issue or maybe a sick child.

When I reached the teacher, she leaned in and whispered:

"I think my granny is... drunk on Nyquil."

I looked over and saw the volunteer completely passed out in a chair — peacefully snoozing during small-group time. The teacher then discreetly pointed to Granny's tote bag, where a bottle of Nyquil was peeking out.

We locked eyes and tried desperately not to laugh — not too loudly, anyway — because the students were very much present and working.

I whispered, "Okay... let's just give her a little nap time."

And so, Granny slept.

And second grade continued.

THE FINAL BELL:

In elementary school, sometimes the students need a break... and sometimes the grown-ups do too.

THE MIKE'S HARDER
SURPRISE

I was once covering a fifth-grade class and needed to grab some materials from the classroom closet. I walked over and tried the handle... locked.

So, I headed to the front office and asked the secretary for the key. She came with me, chatting casually — just a normal school moment.

She opened the door, and we both looked inside.

And then we froze.

Sitting right there on the shelf — in plain view — was a Mike's Harder Lemonade.

A bright, unmistakable adult beverage... inside an elementary school classroom.

Our jaws dropped. We stared at each other in silent panic, trying not to scream, gasp, or make any sound because the students were literally feet away, working quietly at their desks.

As soon as we could breathe again, the hunt began:

Find the principal.

Confirm the discovery.

Begin the investigation.
The irony of it all?
The teacher's last name was Fish.
Drinking like a fish, indeed.

THE FINAL BELL:

In elementary school, you expect to find crayons, glue sticks, and worksheets in a classroom closet — not a plot twist with 8% alcohol by volume.

THAT WOULD BE CRAZY

I was called to a first-grade classroom for a student exhibiting unsafe behaviors. When I walked in, the student was sitting on top of the kidney table — not a great start.

I pulled out every strategy in my toolkit:

"Want to take a walk?"

"No."

"Need a snack?"

"No."

"Want to come sit with me?"

"No."

While I was trying to de-escalate the situation, I heard another student announce— not quietly at all —

"Imagine if they hit the assistant principal. That would be crazy."

I had to bite my lip to keep from laughing.

In my head, all I could think was—

Kid... it happens more often than you think.

Eventually, I took a different angle and said:

"You haven't seen my office yet. Want to come take a look?"

That did the trick. The student climbed down, curiosity winning over chaos.

Later, when I shared the story with my principal, we shared a good, needed laugh after a day filled with challenging behaviors.

Kids have zero awareness of timing — but impeccable comedic delivery.

THE FINAL BELL:

Elementary crises are stressful — but the commentary is unmatched.

THE GREAT PILL SCRAMBLE

It was staff meeting day, and everyone was settling in — notebooks open, caffeine in hand, mentally preparing for the ever-anticipated professional development. Just as things were quieting down, a sudden commotion erupted off to the side of the media center.

We all turned just in time to see a teacher scrambling on the carpet, scooping up small objects with the urgency of someone chasing runaway confetti. Except... it wasn't confetti.

Her medication had spilled everywhere. Pills were rolling under chairs, bouncing off table legs, scattering across the floor like tiny marbles on a mission.

The intensity of her scramble left everyone momentarily stunned, unsure of what exactly was happening — only that she was committed to recovering every single one.

A few of us jumped in to help, offering hands and trying not to laugh at the sheer chaos of the moment. Teaching is demanding, and sometimes the grown-ups bring their own needs into the room right along with their lesson plans.

THE FINAL BELL:

In schools, things fall apart — sometimes even literally — and the staff meeting becomes the scene of an unintended scavenger hunt.

THE HOME VISIT SURPRISE

In one school district I worked in, we kicked off the school year with home visits — teachers and staff visiting students and families a few days before school began. It was a wonderful tradition that helped build relationships... and occasionally delivered a surprise or two.

On one visit, a teacher and our parent liaison arrived at a student's home, rang the doorbell, and waited.

Dad answered the door — and the scene was unforgettable.

His pants were hanging so far below his waist that everyone silently questioned gravity. A wad of cash was spilling out of his pockets like he was mid–music video.

And then, from the back of the house, a woman appeared wearing a skin-tight dress that left absolutely nothing to the imagination about her confidence.

The teacher and liaison exchanged a quick glance — the kind you make when you're trying to decide whether to say "Hello" or just slowly back away.

But they handled it with professionalism, kindness, and a smile, because that's what educators do — even when the home visit feels more like a scene from reality TV.

THE FINAL BELL:

Home visits are meant to help you understand your students' worlds — sometimes they reveal more than you bargained for.

THE MOUSE PROBLEM

Some school buildings are charming because they're old... and some are just old. And with old buildings come old problems — like the kind that scurry.

One year, we found ourselves battling a mouse infestation. Teachers began reporting suspicious snack disappearances — granola bars nibbled, cracker boxes chewed, and entire bags of treats mysteriously light. One teacher finally said, "I swear the mice are eating better than my students."

Then came the moment none of us wanted:

A first-grade teacher walked into her classroom one morning, ready to start the day, only to find a dead mouse in the middle of her rug.

She froze.

We froze when she told us.

And suddenly, everyone in the hallway was walking a little more cautiously.

Old buildings have character, but sometimes that character has whiskers.

THE FINAL BELL:

In schools, you plan lessons for reading and math — pest control is never on the agenda, but it always finds its way in.

THE ROACH FOLDER

The student take-home folder — an iconic staple of parent–teacher communication. It comes back filled with homework, permission slips, notes from home... and, apparently, surprises no one asked for.

One afternoon, a second-grade teacher was checking a student's homework folder during small group instruction. She opened it casually — the same way she had hundreds of times before.

But this time?

Fifteen live roaches came crawling out and scattered across her kidney table like they were late for a meeting.

The teacher screamed.

The students screamed.

Half the hallway probably screamed.

After the chaos settled and her heart rate returned to near normal, she made the dreaded call home — apologizing for startling the student and hoping she hadn't embarrassed them.

The parent responded calmly, as if this were the most normal explanation in the world:

"Oh, we keep his backpack in the garage. That's why."

Mystery solved.

Trauma everlasting.

THE FINAL PELL:

In schools, you brace yourself for forgotten homework, missing permission slips, and snack crumbs — but no teacher is ever emotionally prepared for a folder full of live roaches.

THE RE-GIFTED MAKEUP

Students can be incredibly kind and thoughtful when it comes to gifting their teachers during the holidays. Handmade cards, mugs and homemade cookies — teachers really do see it all.

One day, a fourth-grade teacher came down to my office looking uneasy.

She said, "My student gave me... makeup."

That sounded normal enough — until she added:

"I'm pretty sure it's their mom's."

Sure enough, the child had gone home, found a bag of their mother's makeup, and decided it would make the perfect teacher gift. No wrapping. No note. Just a handful of mom's cosmetics lovingly placed into the teacher's hands.

The teacher felt uncomfortable accepting it, so I made the inevitably awkward call home. I explained gently that her child had "re-gifted" her makeup and that we would be sending it back home in the child's backpack.

The mom was surprised... and slightly amused.

And the teacher breathed a sigh of relief.

THE FINAL BELL:

In elementary school, gifts come from the heart —
even when they also come from Mom's vanity
drawer.

NOT IT

I'm not sure what it is about first grade, but it always seems to be the most rambunctious grade level — full of energy, questionable choices, and bathroom-related adventures no administrator ever asked for.

On this particular day, two boys went to the bathroom together (never a good sign). And in the way only first-grade peer pressure can work, one boy convinced the other to stuff toilet paper into the urinal.

Naturally, the urinal clogged.

Naturally, maintenance was called.

Naturally, the principal emailed home to inform the family.

Fast forward a few weeks.

Another urinal clog.

Another bathroom disaster.

This time, an email to the entire grade level.

The parent, who happened to be on vacation with her son, replied.

Her message was short, confident, and absolutely iconic:

"Not it."

She knew the pattern.

She knew the timing.

And she knew her child was nowhere near that bathroom this time.

THE FINAL BELL:

In elementary school, you don't just manage behaviors — you learn which families respond with "We'll talk to him" and which respond with "Not it."

THE PARA ROOM INVESTIGATION

Sometimes the adults in the building are more dramatic than the kids — and this was one of those times. A paraeducator came to me, clearly frustrated, to report that someone was moving, hiding, or tampering with her belongings in the shared para room.

Each day she'd leave her materials neatly organized... and return to find:
- her chair missing,
- her student work binders gone,
- her papers relocated or hidden.

She suspected someone but didn't want the principal involved yet — especially in case she was wrong. And truthfully, I understood.

So began my independent investigation.

First attempt: a discreet spy camera.

Problem: it wouldn't connect to the school Wi-Fi.

Second attempt: setting up an iPad to record the room when no one was around.

I hid it, positioned it perfectly, hit record, left for a while...

And when I came back?

The iPad was gone.

That's when I knew this was no longer a minor feud — this was turning into a full-blown situation, flirting with police involvement. At that point, I had to loop in the principal.

She sent a building-wide email notifying staff that an iPad had gone missing from the para room and advising everyone not to store personal belongings there until we got answers.

The email worked.

Within minutes, the culprit emailed him wanting to "chat."

The para confessed to taking the iPad — not just taking it but hiding it — because he realized he had been recorded. On camera, he had been:

- ripping down the other para's posted items,

- relocating her materials,
- pulling out her drawer and leaving it on the floor,
- and generally waging a full psychological warfare campaign over the shared space.

When asked why he did all this, his explanation was... extensive.

According to him, the other para had:

- switched his extra pair of shoes so they faced right–left instead of left–right,
- stolen gum from his desk,
- hidden his deodorant,
- and committed an ongoing list of perceived offenses.

It was elementary-school-level drama... but with grown adults.

THE FINAL BELL:

In schools, children aren't the only ones who need conflict resolution — sometimes the staff room requires its own episode of "Dateline."

THE BATHROOM SNAKE

One afternoon, a teacher exited the staff bathroom, and the school secretary went in right after her. As she walked in, she noticed what looked like a ribbon on the floor behind the toilet — long, thin, curled up.

She thought nothing of it.

Did what she needed to do.

Was completely unbothered.

Moments later, another teacher walked in.

Within seconds, the quiet hallway was shattered by a scream so intense it could've signaled the apocalypse.

Because that "ribbon"?

That innocent little strip of something-or-other on the floor?

Was actually a snake.

Cue pandemonium.

Staff running.

Doors slamming.

People shouting "WHERE?!" even though no one actually wanted the answer.

Building Services was called immediately, and they heroically removed the uninvited guest while the rest of us tried to recover from the collective heart attack.

THE FINAL BELL:

In schools, you expect messes in the bathroom — but a snake behind the toilet takes "unexpected visitor" to a whole new level.

MY DAD SAYS

I once had a first grader serving an in-school intervention after a previous day of challenging behaviors. He arrived with the runniest nose imaginable — the kind that drips straight to the top lip. The kind every educator fears.

Trying to be gentle but firm, I said:

"Don't use your clothes to wipe your nose. Let's get a tissue. Then we need to sanitize your hands."

He wiped his nose, tossed the tissue, and I held out the hand sanitizer so I could give him a quick pump.

Without missing a beat, he said:

"My dad says I can't use hand sanitizer."

Okay... curveball.

"Alright," I said, "then let's go to the Health Room and wash your hands with soap."

We walked down, went to the sink, and I held out the soap bottle.

Again—

"My dad says I can't use sanitizer."

I pointed directly at the giant label.

"It says soap."

He looked at it, nodded, and replied with complete seriousness—

"My dad says I can't use soap."

I stared at him.

He stared at me.

All I could think was:

This is going to be a very long day.

At dismissal, I wiped down every surface with disinfectant and silently wondered how this child was out here living a full, soap-less lifestyle.

THE FINAL BELL:

In elementary school, rules vary from home to home — but "no soap" is a plot twist no one is prepared for.

THE HAZMAT PARAEDUCATOR

Ah, COVID-19 — the best of times for the anti-social crowd, and the absolute worst of times for every educator and school administrator trying to keep school functioning.

When in-person instruction finally resumed, staff returned with varying levels of comfort, caution, and... creativity.

One paraeducator arrived ready for anything — and I mean anything.

She walked into the building in a full hazmat suit.

Not just gloves.

Not just a mask.

A full-body, head-to-toe, zippered, hooded, space-exploration-level suit.

And as if that weren't enough, she brought a microphone inside the helmet so students could hear her through the layers of protective gear.

It was wild.

No one knew where to look.

And I honestly could not figure out how she was supposed to do reading interventions when she could barely hear what the students were saying — or what anyone was saying.

But there she was, committed, determined, and fully outfitted for what appeared to be the apocalypse.

THE FINAL BELL:

In post-pandemic schools, PPE came in all levels — from simple masks to full hazmat chic.

THE WAKE-UP
INTERVENTION

Leading a school comes with many responsibilities — some deeply fulfilling, and others that make you wonder how you ended up giving life-coaching advice to fully grown adults.

At one of my schools, we had a staff member who was consistently late. After repeated incidents, the principal and I brought her in for a conversation to understand what was going on.

She sat down, sighed, and said plainly:

"I just can't get up in the morning."

So, there we were — two administrators suddenly transformed into sleep therapists.

"Well, what time do you go to bed?" we asked.

"I am in bed by 8 p.m.," she said confidently.

I blinked.

"So... you're on your phone or watching TV?"

She nodded.

Okay. Progress.

Trying to offer gentle, reasonable solutions, I suggested:

"Have you tried putting your alarm across the room so you have to physically get up to turn it off?"

She said she could try that.

Then the principal jumped in with her own family anecdote.

"My sister has the same problem! She bought this vibrating mat you put under your bed sheets to wake you up."

I nearly died laughing internally.

A vibrating wake-up mat. For adults. Imagine explaining that in HR.

But it didn't stop there.

I remembered that someone once told me about a shock watch — yes, a wearable device that literally shocks you awake unless you solve a puzzle or do a quick physical activity.

So, I asked them for the link.

And, being the responsible administrator I am, I included it in my follow-up email summarizing the meeting.

Because apparently, this is what leadership looks like now.

THE FINAL BELL:

In school administration, you expect to support students — not recommend vibrating bed mats and shock watches to help adults get to work on time. But here we are.

I DIDN'T ENJOY MY TIME

In school leadership, mornings often begin with what I like to call the morning shuffle — figuring out who's absent, where coverage is needed, and how to piece together the day with the personnel available. It's a daily puzzle that rarely has all the pieces.

On this particular day, a Preschool Education Program (PEP) paraeducator was out, so I reassigned a special education para to cover the class. She stepped in, completed the assignment, and the day moved on.

Or so I thought.

Later that evening, I received an email from her requesting a meeting because she "didn't enjoy her time" in the PEP room.

I blinked at my screen.

She wanted a meeting... because she didn't enjoy the task she was assigned.

We met the next morning, and suddenly I was a therapist again. I explained gently — but directly — that we are all part of a team. There are things we all do that we may not love, but we do them because that's what it means to support a school community.

I even said, "Just like I don't particularly enjoy having this conversation right now, here I am — because it's part of my job."

I emphasized flexibility, teamwork, and the importance of stepping in where needed for the collective good of the school.

Still unbelievable that a staff member would tell their supervisor they didn't enjoy a one-day assignment — as if enjoyment were the requirement for doing their job.

THE FINAL BELL:

In leadership, you expect to manage schedules — but you don't expect to explain to grown adults that work isn't always "fun," yet still required.

NEW YEAR, NEW GOALS

The holiday season — a time every educator looks forward to. Along with the festivities comes the annual tradition of reflection, fresh starts, and goal-setting for the new year.

One colleague had her fifth-grade students complete a simple activity:

"My goal for 2026 is..."

The expectations were modest — things like reading more, being kinder, and improving handwriting.

Instead, she got:

"To get my cat a girlfriend."

And right next to it:

"To meet Jake from State Farm."

Hilarious.

Ambitious.

Entirely unrelated to anything realistic or attainable.

The assignment went completely over their heads — and honestly, it made it even better.

THE FINAL BELL:

In elementary school, goals aren't about realism — they're about dreams, cats, and insurance commercials.

THE PINK PONY CLUB

Pink Pony Club — a song I loved deeply. To me, it represented showing up as your true self and living authentically. A few staff members knew how much the song meant to me, especially as I was navigating a difficult transition at work.

One day during fourth- and fifth-grade lunch, I was called down to the cafeteria. When I arrived, the song was playing — for me. Staff had queued it up, kids were smiling, and suddenly we were all singing along, laughing, and just enjoying the moment together.

It was uplifting.

It was fun.

It was one of those rare school moments that fills your cup.

As the song ended, a fifth grader walked up to me and said very matter-of-factly,

"That song is about a strip club."

Without missing a beat, I replied—

"No, it's not."

And then I immediately exited the cafeteria.

Unfortunately, that was not the end.

From that day on, every time I saw that student — in the hallway, at dismissal, during transitions — she would announce loudly, regardless of who was around:

"It's about a strip club."

Parents nearby.

Staff nearby.

Students everywhere.

No filter.

Ever.

THE FINAL BELL:

In elementary school, your meaningful moment will always be followed by a student determined to ruin the vibe with facts they absolutely did not need to share.

THE ART CLASS INCIDENT

Art class — a time for creativity, self-expression, and leaning into one's artistic vibe.

One afternoon, the nurse stopped by my office and said she had a kindergartener in the Health Room who had gotten liquid from Clorox wipes splashed into her eyes.

I froze.

"Who is letting kindergarteners use Clorox wipes?" I asked immediately.

The nurse replied, "She was in art class."

I picked up the phone and called the art teacher right away to find out what had happened. I explained the situation and gently reminded them that students are not allowed to use Clorox wipes.

The response?

"Oh... I didn't know kids weren't allowed to use Clorox wipes."

I paused.

Because to me, it felt like common sense. Give a child a Clorox wipe, and the next thing you know, it's in their eyes, mouth, or being used as a napkin. The outcome seemed painfully obvious.

Thankfully, the student was okay — and that parent too. Imagine making that call!

THE FINAL BELL:

In schools, what feels like common sense isn't always common — especially when cleaning supplies meet kindergarten curiosity.

YOU GET WHAT YOU GET

My first-year teaching third grade — as a career switcher coming from Public Relations — was a complete shock to my system. I had imagined neat rows of desks, students sitting quietly, listening attentively as I delivered beautifully planned lessons.

I was very wrong.

One day, during a class party, I invited my husband to come help out. He was tasked with passing out the most iconic elementary-school snack of all time: fruit snacks.

At the time, Phineas and Ferb was the hottest kids' show, so naturally, there were themed fruit snacks to match. As my husband handed them out, one student — who had a very heavy lisp — kept asking him for something.

I noticed the interaction from across the room and walked over. My husband looked relieved and whispered:

"He's asking for something, and I have no idea what he's saying."

I leaned down and asked, "Baby, what do you need?"

Without hesitation, the student said:

"Phineas and Ferb."

I looked up at my husband, who was still completely puzzled, and said:

"He wants the Phineas and Ferb fruit snacks."

And just like that, it hit me — despite being brand new to teaching, I already knew my students so well that even through a heavy lisp, I understood exactly what he needed.

Then, I turned to my husband and said quietly—

"Also... you messed up."

He looked confused.

"In Teaching 101," I explained, "we don't give kids choices when handing out snacks. You get what you get — and you don't pitch a fit."

Some lessons you learn from textbooks.

Others you learn from fruit snacks.

THE FINAL BELL:

Teaching isn't about perfect plans — it's about knowing your students, speaking their language, and mastering the art of snack distribution.

MIDNIGHT SNACKS

It happens all too often — students falling asleep in class, heads bobbing, eyes barely staying open. One day, I noticed a student nodding off at their desk and gently asked:

"Why are you so tired today?"

Without hesitation, they replied:

"I woke up in the middle of the night."

Concerned, I asked, "Why?"

They looked at me like the answer was obvious and said:

"To have chips and salsa."

I immediately followed up with what every educator would ask:

"Do your parents know you're having midnight snacks?"

They paused.

No answer needed.

THE FINAL BELL:

In elementary school, exhaustion isn't from home-work — it's from poor late-night snack decisions.

THE MASCARA INCIDENT

One afternoon, I spotted a student whose eyelashes looked a little too perfect — dark, dramatic, and very much not naturally enhanced. I invited her over for a closer look, and sure enough... she was wearing mascara.

I asked gently:

"Do your mom and dad know you're wearing mascara?"

Silence.

Which, honestly, answered the question.

I quickly texted her mom to give her a heads-up and included a picture as my receipt. The response came almost instantly:

"Do NOT let her wash it off. Her dad is coming up there right now."

And that's when the full story came out.

She had taken her mom's mascara — you know, the very popular green-and-pink tube — and had been sharing it with friends during lunch.

Dad arrived.

Mascara still intact.
Evidence preserved.

THE FINAL ßELL:

In elementary school, fashion experiments spread fast — and parents appreciate photographic proof.

GROWING A MUSTACHE

Back in my first year of teaching, I had a lot to learn — and one of the hardest lessons was the art of letting go. Letting students move independently. Letting them work without me hovering. Trusting that learning could still happen even when I wasn't directing every moment.

I had received feedback that it was time to try centers. I was told it wouldn't be perfect at first, but that students needed opportunities to collaborate, explore, and learn from one another. Nervous but determined, I carefully planned my centers, explained expectations, and gave it a go.

As I circulated the room, checking in with groups, I overheard one student confidently telling his tablemates:

"I'm working on growing my mustache."

I froze.

At the time, all I could think was:

This is exactly what I was afraid of.

How will they stay on task?

Why are we talking about facial hair?

And no — you are absolutely not growing a mustache in third grade.

I redirected the group and kept moving, but later it hit me: learning doesn't always look like quiet compliance. Sometimes kids need space — not just to think academically, but to be kids.

Centers weren't about perfection.

They were about trust.

THE FINAL BELL:

Not every moment has to be academic — sometimes growth happens when you loosen the reins and let kids just be kids.

MY STOMACH HURTS

There is one excuse that spans grade levels, generations, and decades — the quintessential elementary complaint:

"My stomach hurts."

It's the go-to. The classic. The all-purpose reason to avoid work, tests, or literally anything mildly challenging.

After hearing it enough times, I eventually developed a standard response. I'd say,

"Well, there's really nothing the nurse can do for a hurting stomach. It's not like they can cut it open to see what's wrong."

The students would stare at me, slightly alarmed.

Then I'd continue,

"So you have two options: try to go poop, or drink some water — because in elementary school, water fixes most ailments."

And honestly?

Most of the time, it worked.

THE FINAL BELL:

In elementary school medicine, hydration and a bathroom break solve more problems than you'd expect.

MY STOMACH HURTS
(AGAIN)

Those cute little first graders — endlessly curious and always just one idea away from causing a little trouble. On this particular day, a group of students had already begun the familiar chorus of complaints about the infamous stomachache.

One first grader, clearly taking notes, decided it was his turn. He raised his hand confidently and announced:

"My stomach hurts."

As he said it, he pointed... directly at his throat.

Busted.

We paused, looked at each other, and shared a good laugh. Even he couldn't keep a straight face once he realized the mistake.

THE FINAL BELL:

In first grade, the excuse is practiced — the anatomy, not so much.

PLEASE OPEN IT NOW

The holidays — a time when students love to gift their teachers a little something special. Usually it's a gift card, a candle, or maybe a bottle of their favorite after-school beverage. Thoughtful. Simple. Safe.

And then... there are exceptions.

A colleague once shared that a teacher at their school was gifted three pairs of underwear from Victoria's Secret. As if that weren't surprising enough, the parent insisted that the teacher open the gift in front of the child.

Right there.

No warning.

No alternate plan.

The teacher stood there smiling politely, holding up the package, internally screaming while trying to figure out:

How did they even guess the style?

Let alone the size?

Some gifts are better left wrapped forever.

THE FINAL BELL:

During the holidays, it's truly the thought that counts — but some thoughts should stay at the store.

HERE WE GO AGAIN

I was sitting in my office when the nurse stopped by and said:

"Sara, I have a student in the Health Room who was using a hot glue gun and got burned."

I sighed.

"Whose class were they in?" I asked, already bracing myself.

She replied—

"Art."

And in my head, all I could think was:

Here we go again.

First, it was kindergarteners with Clorox wipes.

Now it was hot glue guns.

I thanked the nurse for letting me know and told her I'd handle it. I immediately sent an email to the teacher explaining that hot glue guns can cause serious burns and that under no circumstances should students be using them.

Somewhere between lesson planning and creativity, basic safety had once again taken a back seat.

THE FINAL BELL:

In schools, creativity is encouraged — but not at the expense of common sense and unburned fingers.

THE HOLIDAY FASHION SHOW

Back to holiday gifts — because educators truly never know what's coming next. A colleague once shared that a teacher at their school received a gift from a family that immediately raised eyebrows: lingerie.

Yes. Lingerie.

As if that alone weren't awkward enough, the story took an unexpected turn. Instead of quietly returning or discreetly re-gifting the item, the teacher decided to lean all the way in.

She put it on... over her clothes... and proceeded to host an impromptu fashion show for her grade-level team.

Thankfully — and this part cannot be emphasized enough — the children were nowhere in sight.

The adults laughed.

The moment passed.

And everyone silently agreed that some gifts come with far too much confidence.

THE FINAL BELL:

During the holidays, teacher gifts are unpredictable — but boundaries are everything, and timing is
key.

A DRESSING DOWN

As a speaker of another language — growing up only allowed to speak Arabic at home and English at school — American sayings sometimes go right over my head. Idioms, especially, have a way of sounding far more dramatic than they actually are.

On one occasion, my principal came into my office and said that a paraeducator was giving the special education teacher a

"Dressing down."

I nodded.

I maintained a serious face.

I acted like I absolutely knew what she meant.

But internally? I was panicking.

A dressing down?

What kind of dressing?

How bad was this situation?

That night, I told my husband:

"You will never believe what my principal came to tell me today, and I have no idea what it means."

He asked what it was, and when I explained, he burst out laughing.

"Babe," he said, "it just means the para was going off on the teacher."

I blinked.

"Oh."

I had definitely imagined something far worse. Another reminder that language — especially idioms — can be tricky when you grow up navigating more than one world.

THE FINAL BELL:

Sometimes leadership isn't about understanding the conflict — it's about first understanding the idiom.

IT'S JUST A COLD

One afternoon, the media specialist sent an email asking to leave early because she wasn't feeling well. It was straightforward — until it wasn't.

Her message read something like this:

She explained that her head congestion had become too much and that she needed to head out early. Then she added, "Funny story before I leave..."

Apparently, the week prior, a Library Leader, who is a student, had been helping her at recess. The student was sniffling, coughing, and reading a book about a foot away from her face. Concerned, the media specialist asked if she was sick.

The student replied confidently:

"No. It's just a cold."

And so, the email concluded with the reassurance that she herself was not sick —

"It's just a cold lol."

The irony was not lost on anyone.

THE FINAL BELL:

In schools, illness is always downplayed — especially when it starts with "It's just a cold."

SCHWEDDY BALLS

It was the first morning back after a break, and I was making my usual rounds — popping into classrooms, saying hello to students and teachers, and soaking in the post-break energy.

When I walked into a fourth-grade classroom, the teacher had students reflecting on their time off using sticky notes. They were writing about something they did, someone they saw, and somewhere they went.

One student wrote that she had visited the Ben & Jerry's Factory in Vermont. Naturally, the teacher followed up with a question that made perfect sense, given the context:

"What's one flavor you saw?"

Without hesitation, the student announced loudly and confidently,

"Schweddy Balls."

The teacher and I locked eyes and froze.

Then we both completely lost it.

Her face turned bright red.

I laughed so hard I had to excuse myself and said:

"I think I'm going to go now."

Still, the damage was done.

We laughed about it all day — and honestly, we still laugh about it to this day.

THE FINAL BELL:

Sometimes reflection activities uncover memories... and sometimes, they uncover words you were absolutely not prepared to hear in a fourth-grade classroom.

BUSTED MY ASS

On the day I broke my nose, I texted my principal to give him a heads-up about my appearance. Despite the injury, I fully planned on coming to school the next day — broken nose and all.

I texted him:

"Mr. Burns, I busted my ass at the bike park."

He replied enthusiastically:

"Nice! I've spent the last eight hours busting my butt deep-cleaning this house."

Clearly, he thought I was speaking figuratively.

I was not.

Realizing the disconnect, I followed up quickly:

"Don't judge me — I broke my nose."

That's when the tone shifted. Apologies followed, along with:

"Didn't you get the memo that says you can't ride bikes when you're over 40?"

We both laughed — and I showed up the next day with a swollen face and a great story.

THE FINAL BELL:

In leadership, even serious injuries can turn into comedy — especially when texting leaves room for interpretation.

HANDSOME DAN

I once worked at a school where many staff members also had their own children enrolled — myself included. It made for a tight-knit community where work life and family life blended in ways you never quite expect.

One morning, after finishing a 504 meeting, I began my usual rounds. I stopped into a second-grade classroom and casually said to the teacher:

"I just saw your husband."

It took her a second to process why I would've just seen him — and then, out of nowhere, one of her students blurted out:

"Handsome Dan?"

The teacher's face immediately turned bright red.

I froze for half a second... and then we both burst out laughing.

Clearly, that nickname had made its way into the classroom vocabulary — whether intentionally or not.

THE FINAL BELL:

In elementary school, students don't just learn academics — they also pick up everything you didn't realize you shared.

COP WITH GRANDMA

One afternoon, a situation at school escalated quickly and required police involvement. It was the kind of day that stretched on forever — paperwork, phone calls, and staying at school well past dismissal, close to 6:00 p.m.

Our admin secretary was out that day, leaving just the attendance secretary holding things down with us. Earlier, she had shared that she had an appointment and wouldn't be able to stay late. In a brief lull during the chaos, I sent her a quick text letting her know she was free to go.

Her response came back almost immediately:

"No, I'm good. Listening to the cop talking to grandma. He has big muscles."

I stared at my phone and burst out laughing. In the middle of stress and uncertainty, she was fully tuned into the muscles of the officer explaining things to his grandmother.

It was a reminder I didn't know I needed.

THE FINAL BELL:

Even on the hardest days, a little humor — and a lot of muscles — can lighten the moment.

THE FURRIES

As my son entered his middle school era, he was quickly introduced to a brand-new reality: middle school is a time for figuring out who you want to be in the world — and sometimes that identity changes day to day... or even minute to minute.

One afternoon, he came home completely stunned. He shared that some students in his class were wearing cat tails — actual tails. As he observed more closely, he learned that this group referred to themselves as furries and communicated with one another through purrs — during class.

We all shared a good laugh. For a while after that, it became a running family joke — casually checking in and asking, "So... how are the furries doing?"

The humor wasn't in judgment, but in the realization that middle school is where individuality shows up loudly, unapologetically, and sometimes with accessories.

Welcome to adolescence.

THE FINAL BELL:

Middle school is less about fitting in and more about figuring out who you are — even if that includes a tail and a purr.

THE KITCHEN TABLE

Administration can be a lonely job. There's a constant balancing act — being a supervisor while still building relationships, staying connected but not too connected. That's where the relationship between an Assistant Principal and Principal becomes essential.

It's the one person who truly understands the job. The one person you can vent to. The one person who gets the pressures, the politics, and the moments no one else sees. Over time, stories are shared — and many laughs are had.

On one occasion, my principal shared a story from his own journey to the principalship, back when he was completing his internship. One afternoon, he received a text from a staff member that read:

"Meet me naked at the kitchen table."

The problem?

The text was very much intended for the staff member's wife — and very much sent to his very male principal instead.

Talk about awkward. For both of them.

Years later, the embarrassment has faded, but the story — and the laughter — still lives on.

THE FINAL BELL:

Sometimes leadership means managing crises... and sometimes it means surviving a text that was never meant for you.

THE BATHROOM CHECK-IN

One of my principals — who began their career as a kindergarten teacher — once shared a story that would make anyone laugh for a long time to come. If you've ever taught kindergarten, you know the small victories: one of the biggest being a bathroom inside the classroom.

One day, a male student asked to use the restroom. Minutes passed. Then more minutes. Longer than average. Concerned, the teacher knocked gently and called out,

"[Student name], are you okay?"

No response.

After a little more time passed, the teacher knocked again, firmer this time.

"[Student name], you need to open the door."

When the door finally opened, the teacher immediately realized this was not a routine situation. The student had gone number two and, in an earnest attempt to clean himself, had turned the bathroom into a full-blown disaster.

Without hesitation — and without panic — the teacher calmly said,

"Pull up your pants. We're going to the nurse."

Because sometimes, professionalism means moving forward and never looking back.

THE FINAL BELL:

Kindergarten teachers don't flinch — they problem-solve, redirect, and call the nurse.

MEET THE AUTHOR

Sara Ajisafe is an educator, school leader, and lifelong storyteller with over a decade of experience in elementary education across three states and five school districts. A former Public Relations professional turned classroom teacher, Sara has served as a third-grade teacher, Assistant Principal, and Acting Principal, where she became known for her calm leadership, deep empathy for students, and ability to find humor in even the most unexpected moments.

Throughout her career, Sara has worked closely with students, families, and staff, navigating everything from playground investigations to front-office surprises — experiences that inspired this collection of true stories. She believes that schools are some of the most human places on Earth, filled with honesty, laughter, big emotions, and unforgettable lessons.

Sara currently serves in school leadership and is passionate about creating safe, joyful learning environments where students feel seen, valued, and supported. When she's not in a school hallway or writing, she enjoys spending time with her husband and two sons, documenting life's moments, and laughing at the things kids say when they think no one is listening.

Thank you for reading her first book.